Terrific Trucks!

SEMI TRUCKS

Ursula Pang

PowerKiDS press

PK Beginners

Here come
semi trucks!

Semi trucks
move things
from place to place.

The front part
is the tractor.

A worker drives the tractor.

The tractor pulls the trailer.

The trailer carries a load.

This semi truck takes food to stores.

FOOD LION
FOOD LION
FOLLOW
ME TO
FRESH
& AFFORDABLE
foodlion.com
22301023

The semi truck moves potatoes.

This semi truck moves farm animals.

This semi truck
is moving a house!

OVERSIZE LOAD

This semi truck is moving other semi trucks!

Published in 2026 by The Rosen Publishing Group, Inc.
2544 Clinton Street, Buffalo, NY 14224

First Edition

Editor: Greg Roza
Book Design: Jeffrey Taylor

Photo Credits: Cover Vitpho/Shutterstock.com; p. 3 Vitpho/Shutterstock.com; p. 5 Andrei Mayatnik/Shutterstock.com; p. 7 Vitpho/Shutterstock.com; p. 9 maxbelchenko/Shutterstock.com; p. 11 Siwakorn1933/Shutterstock.com; p. 13 aapskyShutterstock.com; p. 15 refrina/Shutterstock.com; p. 17 StockStudio Aerials/Shutterstock.com; p. 19 Miguel Perfectti/Shutterstock.com; p. 21 Henryk Sadura/Shutterstock.com; p. 23 Vitpho/Shutterstock.com.

Cataloging-in-Publication Data

Names: Pang, Ursula.
Title: Semi trucks / Ursula Pang.
Description: Buffalo, New York : PowerKids Press, 2026. | Series: Terrific trucks! | Includes glossary and index.
Identifiers: ISBN 9781499451733 (pbk.) | ISBN 9781499451740 (library bound) | ISBN 9781499451757 (ebook)
Subjects: LCSH: Tractor trailer combinations--Juvenile literature. | Truck trailers--Juvenile literature.
Classification: LCC TL230.15 P36 2026 | DDC 629.224--dc23

Manufactured in the United States of America

CPSIA Compliance Information: Batch #CSPK26. For further information contact Rosen Publishing at 1-800-237-9932.